This book is dedicated to the two people who make up my entire universe. To my husband and best friend, Kyle, thank you for encouraging me to pursue my dreams and never telling me they are silly or out of reach. I love you more. To our daughter, Clara, may you always find the courage to pursue every adventure your heart seeks out. I will forever be your biggest supporter. You are my heart and joy.

Giraffes in Outer Space

Story by Christine Melaas

Illustrations by Karen Kalbacher

It was the first day of school for Zippy. His mother had packed his favorite lunch, along with his school supplies in his brand new rocket ship backpack.

Zippy loved space. Zippy dreamed of growing so tall that he would be able to see every star in the sky. This dream, however, seemed as far away as the Milky Way. Zippy was not as tall as other giraffes his age. His neck just had not quite sprouted.

As Zippy headed out the door, Mother kissed him and called out, "Good luck my special giraffe. I love you!"

Inside the schoolhouse, all of the students had begun taking their seats. Zippy looked around for somewhere to sit. As his eyes made their way around the classroom, he noticed a grey trunk waving him over to an empty desk.

The trunk belonged to an elephant who introduced himself as, "Eli elephant. Nice to meet you. You can sit here by me!"

"Hi," said Zippy timidly. "Thank you. Nice to meet you, too.

Mr.

"Welcome to your first day of school, students!" Greeted Mr. Leon. "Let's go around the room and introduce ourselves. Please say your name and share an interesting fact about yourself."

When it came to be Zippy's turn, he looked down at the floor and in a shy voice said, "Um, hello. My name is Zippy. When I grow up, I want to go to outer space.

Behind Zippy, another much taller giraffe chuckled and teased, "Ha! Whoever heard of a giraffe in outer space?"

"Now, now class. Settle down, please. Anything is possible!" Mr. Leon said as he smiled and winked at Zippy.

At Recess, Zippy overheard the other giraffes still laughing in a circle about his answer. Why did I have to say that? Thought Zippy to himself as tears welled up in his eyes. He ran out of the schoolyard and hid behind a shed where no one would see him crying.

As Zippy sat there sniffling he heard a familiar voice. It was Eli. "Are you okay, Zippy?" Eli asked.

"I guess. I just wish I were like everyone else. Then the other kids wouldn't make fun of me." Replied Zippy.

Shrugging his shoulders Eli said, "I know how you feel."

"You do?" Zippy asked.

"Yes. My cousins are always teasing me because of my trunk. Elephants are supposed to be strong and use our trunks to be handy like helping to lift heavy objects. But, I'm not very handy or strong."

Zippy looked at Eli. It was the first time he had met someone who understood what it felt like to not be the same as everyone else. "Wow. I had no idea, Eli. Well, I think you're great! You made me feel welcome in class when no one else did. That's a pretty strong elephant in my book!"

Eli and Zippy smiled at one another. Just as Zippy was about to suggest they head back to the schoolyard, they heard a loud

CRASH! ZING! ZOOM!

And what sounded like someone or something shrieking for help. They turned around and saw a cloud of smoke coming from a nearby bush. Zippy and Eli ran over to check out what they had heard.

As the two new friends approached the cloud of smoke, out of the bush came a tiny, blue... Martian! He was wobbling as he walked and talking to himself in weird sounds. Finally, the blue Martian looked up realizing he wasn't alone. The three stopped, stared at each other and "AHHHHHH!" they screamed trying to run away, but they all ran right into each other.

"Ohhhh, I'm seeing stars and they're not from my backyard." Moaned the Martian.

"Wh-wha-who are you?" Eli spouted out.

The blue Martian stood up, dusted himself off and said, "Pleased to meet you both. I'm Funkertickelnoodle, but everyone at home calls me Funky. I come from the Milky Way, where I should be right now passing my driver's test. Instead, I took a wrong turn, and seemed to have crashed my spaceship on Earth. I don't know what I'm going to do. I have to get back!"

Zippy couldn't believe his eyes. A Martian from the Milky Way was standing in front of them. "It's amazing to meet you, Funky! I'm Zippy, and this is my friend, Eli. Hey! You know, Eli is handy. Maybe he can try fixing your spaceship?"

"Um, Zippy?" Whispered Eli to Zippy. "You know I can't fix things. I just told you-," Zippy interrupted Eli.

"Sure you are! Maybe you just haven't found what you're handy at fixing. This might be it!"

Eli got a look of confidence on his face when Zippy said that. "Well, I mean, maybe I could take a look at it for you."

"I'm willing to give it a whirl if you are!" Exclaimed Funky.

Eli got to work right away. While he tinkered with the spaceship, Zippy and Funky stood by watching.

"You know, I always thought Martians were green," Zippy said to Funky.

"Yes, well, they are. That's why everyone calls me Funky because my blue color is funky compared to the other green Martians."

Zippy smiled and thought, it looks like Earth isn't the only place where you can feel different. "I think your color is better than any Martian's color I've ever seen in books."

That was the first time someone had accepted Funky for who he was and not what color he was. "Thank you, Zippy! That means the universe to me!"

As the two exchanged a kind look, Eli shouted, "I think I did it!"

All of a sudden, Funky's spaceship started humming and pinging while its lights flashed brilliant colors of red and green.

"Eli you did it! You are the handiest elephant in any galaxy I have ever come across!" Funky hugged Eli's trunk with excitement. "Thank you so much!"

Who knew? Thought Eli. I just might be handy after all.

"Well friends, I have to be on my way. It's been the crash of a lifetime meeting you both." Funky gathered up his things and started getting into his spaceship.

"You sure are lucky to live in space." Said Zippy looking up at the sky. "I dream of going there someday."

"Well, why not come take a spin with me? I think I can spare a few more minutes for my new friends who saved the day!"

Zippy gasped, "Really? But, how?"

Funky hopped out and pulled out a helmet attached to a long hose. "Like this!" He floated up and put the helmet on Zippy's head, and then he attached the hose to his backpack. "Tada! I bet you didn't know your backpack was actually a spacesuit."

Zippy's dream was about to come true. Funky thanked Eli again for his handy help, buckled up, revved up his engine and they were off! Zippy was actually zipping through the sky next to Funky. Higher and higher, they got until they were floating above the Earth.

Funky told Zippy it was time to head back home. With a flash of light, they entered Earth and Zippy found himself back in the school-yard. Eli was there waiting. As Funky hovered above his new friends, he called out, "Thank you for all your help and for showing me being different is great!" Then he zoomed off back into the stars.

Eli and Zippy waved goodbye. Smiling at one another, they knew their lives had changed that day. After all, who else could say they fixed a blue Martian's spaceship and got to visit outer space during recess? With that, they headed into their classroom, ready for their next adventure.

Made in the USA
Coppell, TX
20 February 2020

16039578R00036